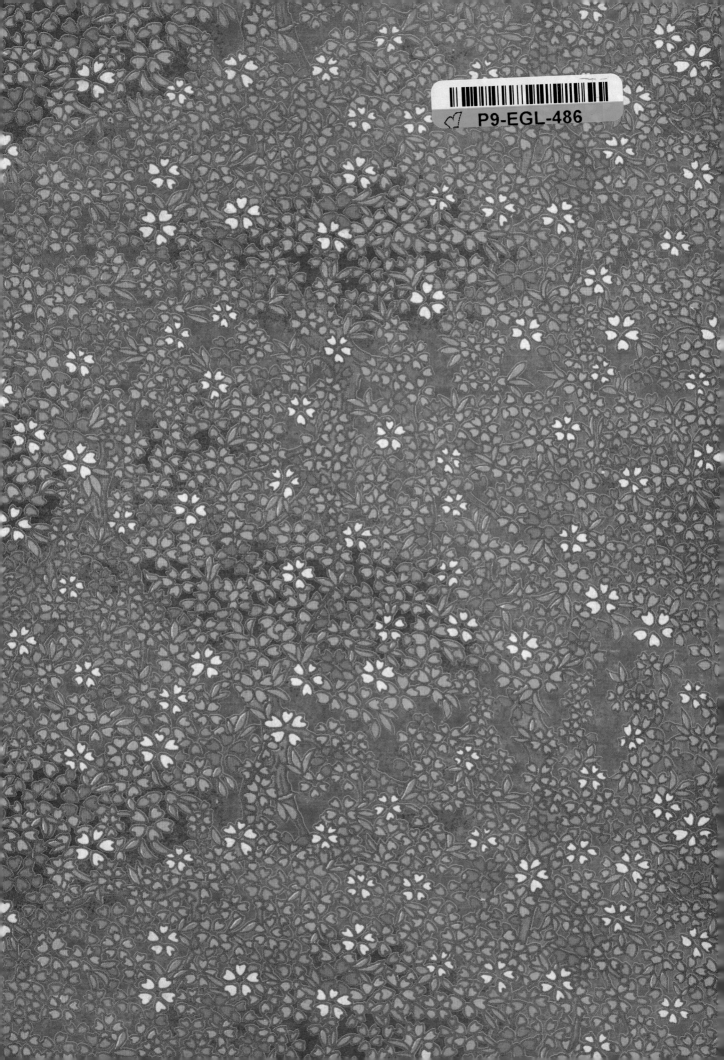

P9-EGL-486

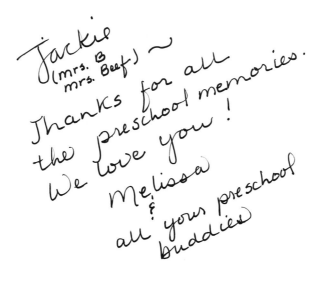

Jackie
(mrs. B
mrs. Beef) ~

Thanks for all
the preschool memories.
We love you !
Melissa
&
all your preschool
buddies

THIS IS MY WISH FOR YOU

TEXT BY CHARLES LIVINGSTON SNELL

COMPILED BY HAROLD DARLING

BORDERS BY DANIEL MACLISE, R.A.

LAUGHING ELEPHANT BOOKS

2000

COPYRIGHT © 1992, BLUE LANTERN STUDIO. ALL RIGHTS RESERVED.
TENTH PRINTING. PRINTED IN HONG KONG.
ISBN 0-9621131-4-X

LAUGHING ELEPHANT BOOKS
PO BOX 4399 · SEATTLE · WASHINGTON
98104-0399

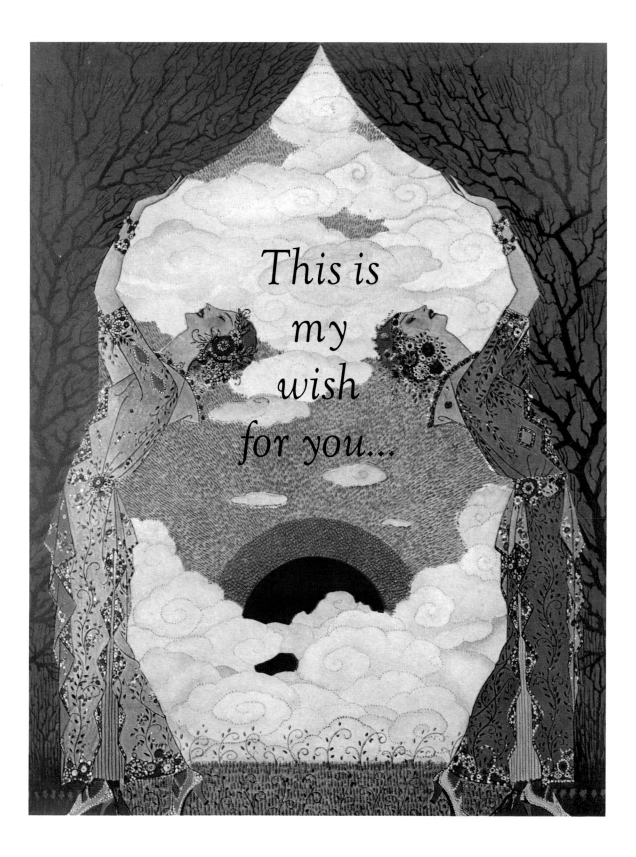

This is
my
wish
for you...

That the spirit
of beauty
may continually
hover about you
and fold
you close within
the tendernesses
of her wings.

That each
beautiful
and gracious
thing in life
may be unto you
as a symbol
of good for your
soul's delight.

That sun-glories

7

and
star-glories

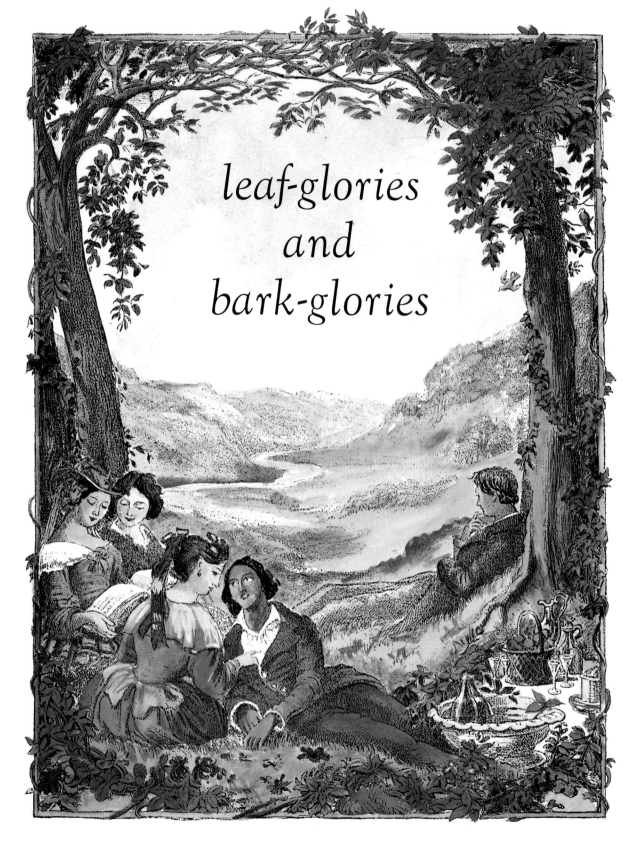

leaf-glories
and
bark-glories

11

flower-glories

and glories
that lurk
in the grasses
of the field

glories of
mountains

17

and
oceans

*of little streams
of running
waters*

21

glories
of song

23

of poesy

of all
the arts

27

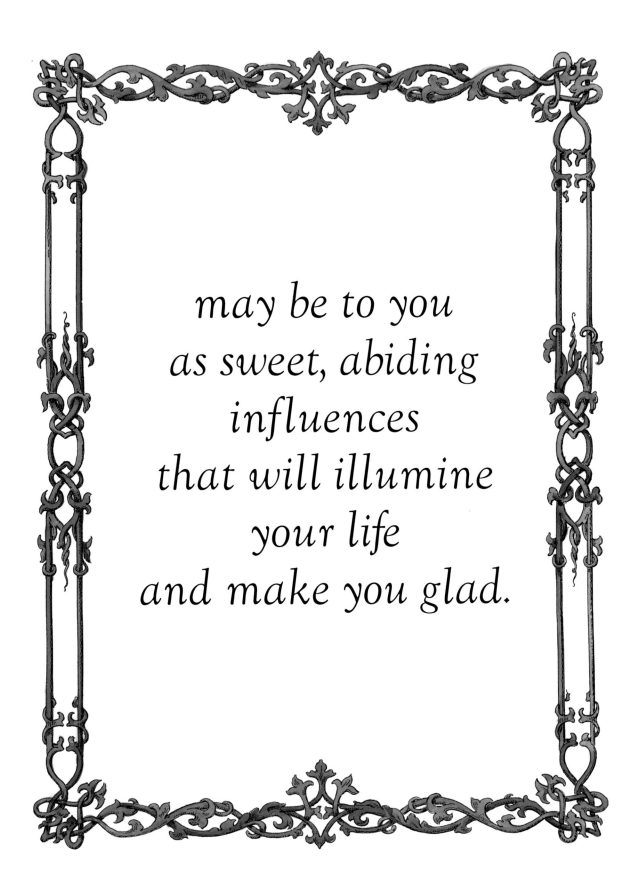

may be to you
as sweet, abiding
influences
that will illumine
your life
and make you glad.

29

That your soul
may be as
an alabaster cup,
filled to
overflowing with
the mystical wine
of beauty
and love.

That happiness
may put
her arms
around you,

33

and wisdom
make
your soul serene.

This is
my wish
for you.

THIS BOOK WAS DESIGNED AND SET IN GOUDY OLDSTYLE BY
THE BLUE LANTERN STUDIO.

PICTURE CREDITS

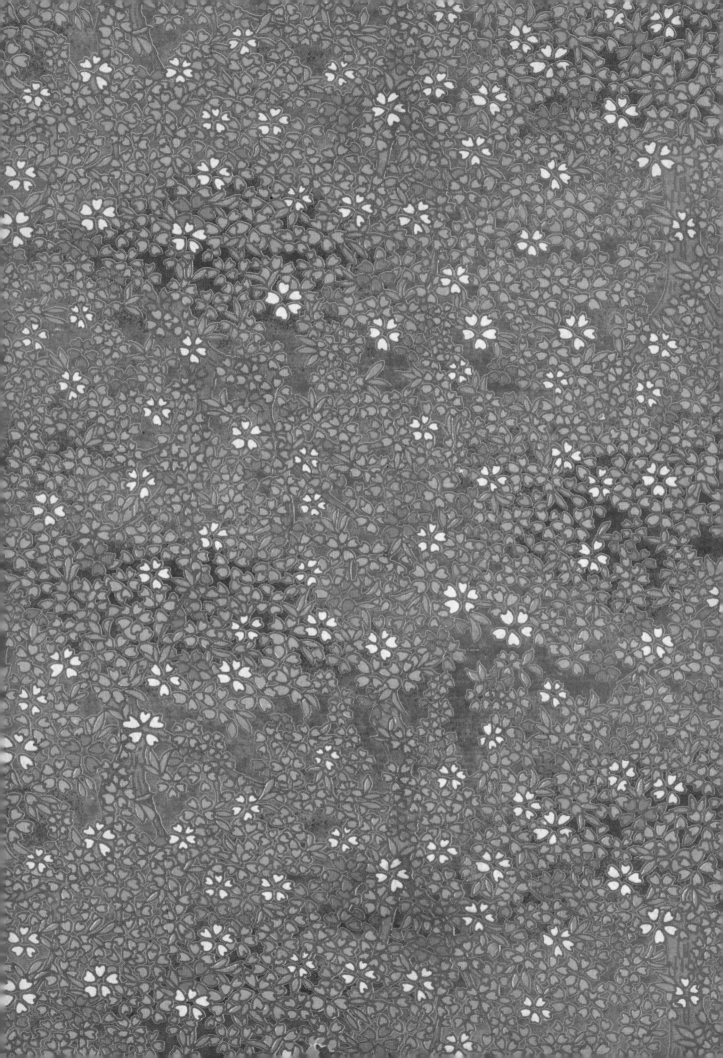